Thrive: The Next Chapter of Human Motivation

By Michael McCarthy

First Edition

"A bold vision for systems of abundance, interdependence, and resilience."

Thrive: The Next Chapter of Human Motivation © 2024, Michael McCarthy

All rights reserved.

No part of this publication may be reproduced, distributed, or transmitted in any form or by any means, including photocopying, recording, or other electronic or mechanical methods, without the prior written permission of the publisher, except in the case of brief quotations embodied in critical reviews and certain other noncommercial uses permitted by copyright law. For permission requests, contact the publisher at michaelrhettmccarthy@gmail.com.

Self-Published by Michael McCarthy

First Edition: 2024

Published in Greenville, South Carolina

ISBN: 9798302963413

Disclaimer

This book is based on personal experiences, research, and interpretations. It is intended to provide general information and does not constitute professional advice. Readers are encouraged to seek appropriate guidance for their unique circumstances.

Design and Formatting

Cover design and interior formatting by Michael McCarthy

Acknowledgments

Special thanks to Brian Stears for believing in me when I couldn't believe in myself.

Thrive: The Next Chapter of Human Motivation

Preface: From Strive to Thrive..8
Chapter 1: Survival to Strive...11
The Rise of Motivation 2.0..12
The Legacy of Strive..13
A Personal Reflection..13
Motivation 2.0: A Flawed Operating System..16
The Zoo: Controlled Freedom..17
The Consequences of Constraint..18
A Personal Reflection..19
Chapter 3: The Fish and the Tree..21
The Limits of Standardized Metrics..21
The Cost of Marginalization...22
A Personal Reflection..23
The Fish in the Wild..24
Chapter 4: Why Drive Alone Isn't Enough..26
The Hardware Problem...26
The Illusion of Freedom..27
The Cost of Conformity...28
A Glimpse of the Wild...28
The Promise of Thrive...29
Chapter 5: Strive Under Fear – Control, Conformity, and Subversion............31
McCarthyism and the Lavender Scare..31
The Personal Cost of Fear-Driven Systems..32
Control vs. Creativity..33
The Courage to Subvert..33
A Glimpse of the Wild...34
Chapter 6: Pathological Demand Avoidance and the Pariah Problem...........36
The Demand for Compliance...36
The Creativity of Resistance..37
The Cost of Marginalization...38

Thrive and the Pariah Problem..38
A Reflection on Resistance...39
Chapter 7: The Cost of Strive.. 41
The Psychological Toll.. 41
The Social Cost..42
The Creativity Deficit...43
The Cost of Disconnection...43
A Reflection on Cost... 44
A Glimpse of Thrive...44
Chapter 8: The Principles of Thrive..................................... 47
Abundance: Moving Beyond Scarcity.................................. 47
Interdependence: The Strength of Connection.................. 48
Resilience: Thriving Through Change..................................49
The Promise of Thrive...50
A Reflection on Principles..50
Chapter 9: Rewilding Education..53
The Constraints of Standardization......................................53
The Zoo of Controlled Learning.. 54
The Wild: A New Vision for Education................................. 55
A Personal Reflection... 55
The Promise of Rewilding..56
Chapter 10: Rewilding the Economy....................................58
The Scarcity Mindset.. 58
The Problem of Growth..59
The Zoo of Managed Economies... 60
The Wild: A New Vision for Economies...............................60
A Personal Reflection... 61
The Promise of Rewilding... 61
Chapter 11: Breaking Free of Strive Metrics...................... 64
The Tyranny of Metrics... 64
The Cost of Over-Measurement... 65

The Growth Mindset	66
Redefining Success	66
A Personal Reflection	67
The Promise of Breaking Free	67
Chapter 12: The Role of AI in Thrive	70
AI in Strive Systems	70
AI in Thrive Systems	71
The Risks of AI in Thrive	72
Personal Reflections on AI	72
The Wild Potential of AI	73
A Call to Action	73
Chapter 13: Emotional Resilience and Collective Striving	76
The Role of Emotional Resilience	76
The Cost of Isolation	77
The Power of Collective Striving	77
Resilience in the Wild	78
A Personal Reflection	79
The Promise of Collective Resilience	79
Chapter 14: Returning to the Commons	82
The Erosion of the Commons	82
The Power of the Commons	83
Reclaiming the Commons	83
A Personal Reflection	84
A Call to Reclaim	85
Chapter 15: The Lion's Roar	87
Balancing Autonomy, Mastery, and Belonging	87
The Collective Roar	88
A Reflection on Belief	89
The Call to Thrive	90
Epilogue: The Thrive Collective	92
The Power of Community and Belief	92

The Parallels to My Story..93
The Thrive Collective: A Vision for the Future...93
An Invitation to Join..94
A Personal Reflection..94
The Final Call to Thrive...95
References...97

Preface: From Strive to Thrive

For much of human history, the driving force behind our actions has been survival. We hunted, gathered, and toiled, ensuring we could eat another meal, live another day. But as societies evolved, survival wasn't enough. We wanted more. So, we built systems—frameworks to organize our work, our learning, and our communities. These systems promised efficiency, security, and progress. They pushed us to strive for goals bigger than ourselves.

Yet, over time, these systems became their own masters. They morphed into rigid structures that rewarded compliance and punished deviation. They valued control over creativity, output over well-being, and scarcity over abundance. In the pursuit of progress, we lost sight of what it truly means to thrive.

This book is a call to reconsider the systems that shape our lives. Drawing from the work of brilliant thinkers—Daniel Pink, Howard Gardner, Michel Foucault, Aldo Leopold, and many others—it explores the limitations of what I call **Strive systems**, those built on the principles of Motivation 2.0: control, fear, and scarcity. It challenges us to imagine what comes after: **Thrive systems**, rooted in abundance, interdependence, and resilience.

For me, this journey is deeply personal. There was a time when I believed I had succeeded in navigating the very systems I critique in this book. I worked hard, met the metrics society demanded of me, and achieved what seemed like stability. But then, life took a turn.

I began experiencing strange and debilitating health symptoms—dizziness, pain, and exhaustion that wouldn't go away. Doctor after doctor dismissed me, misdiagnosed me, or gave me no answers at all. For years, I struggled with the fear and uncertainty of not knowing what was happening to my body. It wasn't until much later that I discovered I was likely living with Ehlers-Danlos Syndrome (EDS) and Postural Orthostatic Tachycardia Syndrome (POTS), conditions that are still misunderstood and often ignored by the medical system.

This was when I began to question the very foundations of the systems I had trusted. Why did a system designed to heal feel so dehumanizing? Why was I treated as a set of symptoms to be managed rather than a person to be cared for? And why, when I could no longer meet society's metrics of productivity, did I feel invisible?

At the same time, I was coming to terms with my neurodivergence. Diagnosed with ADHD later in life, and recognizing my profile as autistic with PDA (Pathological Demand Avoidance), I began to see how the traits that made me who I am—my creativity, my need for autonomy, my resistance to conformity—were seen as problems in a world built for compliance.

The more I reflected, the more I saw the connections between my personal experiences and the broader systemic issues we face as a society. Our education systems demand standardized success. Our workplaces value output over well-being. Our economies thrive on competition and scarcity. These are Strive systems, and they are failing us.

But it doesn't have to be this way. Inspired by the work of Daniel Pink, I began to think about what comes after Motivation 3.0, his model built on **autonomy, mastery, and purpose**. While Pink's framework offers a powerful blueprint for individual motivation, I realized it wasn't enough to change the larger systems. To truly thrive, we need to rethink the systems themselves.

In this book, I propose a framework for **Motivation 4.0**—a shift from **Strive** to **Thrive**. Thrive systems are built on three principles:

- **Abundance**: A rejection of the scarcity mindset that underpins Strive systems.
- **Interdependence**: Recognizing that no one thrives alone and that connection is a source of strength.

- **Resilience**: Designing systems that adapt and grow stronger through change and adversity.

As you read, you'll see the metaphors of **The Farm, The Zoo, and The Wild** woven throughout. These landscapes represent the systems we've built: the farm as a place of control, the zoo as a place of constrained freedom, and the wild as a place of interdependence and growth. I use these metaphors not just as academic tools, but as reflections of my own journey—of moving from systems that constrained me to spaces where I could begin to thrive.

This book is both a critique of the systems we've inherited and an invitation to imagine something better. It draws on the wisdom of scholars across disciplines—economics, psychology, education, sociology, and ecology—and connects their insights to the deeply human desire to flourish.

It is my hope that as you read, you'll reflect on your own experiences with these systems. Where have you felt the weight of Strive? Where have you glimpsed the possibility of Thrive? And most importantly, what role can you play in building systems that allow all of us to flourish—not just survive, not just strive, but truly thrive?

This is the promise of **Thrive**. Let's begin.

Chapter 1: Survival to Strive

At the dawn of humanity, survival was our singular focus. We hunted, foraged, and adapted to a world that offered no guarantees. Motivation 1.0, as Daniel Pink describes it, was simple and primal: the need to eat, reproduce, and avoid danger. In these early days, we lived as part of the wilderness, dependent on the rhythms of nature and the strength of our communities.

But as humans began to cultivate the land, something shifted. We transitioned from hunters and gatherers to farmers and settlers, trading the uncertainty of the wild for the predictability of the farm. This was the beginning of domestication—not just of plants and animals, but of ourselves. We moved from systems built on cooperation and abundance to systems that prioritized control and scarcity.

James C. Scott, in his book *Seeing Like a State*, explores this transformation in detail. He argues that domestication was humanity's first act of systemic control. By organizing land into plots, animals into pens, and people into roles, we created a world that was more efficient but also more constrained. In many ways, this marked the birth of **Strive systems**: systems built to optimize productivity, reward compliance, and minimize risk.

As I reflect on this shift, I can't help but think about how much my own life has mirrored this story. For much of my early life, I bought into the idea that the key to success was mastering the rules of the system. I worked hard to meet the metrics—whether it was grades in school, performance reviews at work, or societal expectations about what success should look like. And for a while, it seemed to work. I was, in a sense, thriving within the farm.

But just like the early farmers who became dependent on the stability of their crops, I realized how fragile this system truly was. When my health began to fail, the very structures I had relied on—the workplace, the healthcare system, even the safety net I thought existed—began to crumble. Suddenly, I wasn't a person anymore. I was a problem to be solved, a body that didn't fit the system's neatly designed molds.

This is the danger of Strive systems: they value control over creativity, output over well-being, and efficiency over humanity. Aldo Leopold, the great environmentalist, once said, "We abuse the land because we regard it as a commodity belonging to us." The same could be said of how we treat one another. Strive systems commodify people, measuring their worth by their productivity and their ability to conform.

The Rise of Motivation 2.0

Motivation 2.0—the system of rewards and punishments—is the software that powered this new way of life. If Motivation 1.0 was about survival, Motivation 2.0 was about control. It introduced the carrot and the stick: incentives to drive behavior, punishments to enforce compliance.

This system worked, at least for a time. It helped build empires, fuel industrial revolutions, and drive progress on a scale humanity had never seen before. But it came at a cost. By reducing people to their utility—to what they could produce or achieve—Motivation 2.0 stifled the very qualities that make us human: creativity, curiosity, and connection.

I've felt this cost personally. Growing up, I was often praised for being a "hard worker," for my ability to meet deadlines and exceed expectations. But as I got older, I began to realize how narrow these metrics were. They didn't capture my creativity, my need for autonomy, or my drive to explore ideas that didn't fit neatly into a box. And when I started experiencing symptoms of EDS and

POTS, these systems had no room for someone like me. I wasn't seen as a person anymore—I was seen as a deviation, a problem to be managed.

The Legacy of Strive

The legacy of Strive systems is all around us. We see it in our education systems, which prioritize standardized testing over curiosity and creativity. We see it in our workplaces, which reward efficiency over innovation. And we see it in our economies, which thrive on competition and scarcity rather than collaboration and abundance.

Albert Einstein once said, "We cannot solve our problems with the same thinking we used when we created them." And yet, that's exactly what Strive systems ask us to do. They ask us to keep working harder, to keep striving, even when it's clear that the system itself is broken.

This is why I believe we need a new framework—a shift from Strive to Thrive. Thrive systems recognize that the goal of life isn't just to survive or even to strive, but to flourish. They prioritize abundance, interdependence, and resilience, creating conditions where both individuals and communities can reach their full potential.

A Personal Reflection

As I write this, I think about how much my own journey has shaped my understanding of these systems. I think about the doctors who dismissed my symptoms because they didn't fit neatly into their checklists. I think about the teachers who encouraged me to conform rather than celebrate my unique way of thinking. And I think about the moments when I felt like giving up because I couldn't see a way forward.

But I also think about the people who believed in me—friends like Brian Stearns, who gave me shelter and support when I had nowhere else to turn. Their belief reminded me of something Les Brown once said: "Other people's opinions of you do not have to become your reality." This truth has stayed with me, guiding me as I navigate a world that often feels more like a farm or a zoo than a wild and thriving ecosystem.

In the chapters ahead, we'll explore what it means to move from Strive to Thrive. We'll look at the systems that constrain us and the possibilities that emerge when we reimagine them. And we'll see how, together, we can build a world where thriving isn't just possible—it's inevitable.

Chapter 2: The Software of Strive

Motivation 2.0, the system of rewards and punishments, has become the default operating system of our modern world. It powers our schools, workplaces, and economies, shaping how we measure success and how we define our worth. Like a piece of outdated software, it still functions, but it's riddled with bugs. It crashes under the weight of complexity, stifling creativity, and innovation.

The metaphors of **The Farm and The Zoo** help us understand this system. The Farm is where control is absolute, and freedom is non-existent. The Zoo offers a simulation of freedom—more choices, more safety—but within tightly controlled boundaries. Both are systems of constraint, designed to optimize efficiency rather than foster growth.

I've lived in both of these systems. In school, I was the fish that Albert Einstein talked about—the one being judged by its ability to climb a tree. The curriculum, the tests, the metrics—they were all designed for a particular type of learner. For a long time, I thought my struggles were a reflection of my own shortcomings. But looking back now, I see how much the system itself was at fault. It wasn't designed to recognize or celebrate the kind of thinker I am.

Motivation 2.0: A Flawed Operating System

Daniel Pink describes Motivation 2.0 as the carrot-and-stick approach to motivation. It assumes that people are fundamentally driven by rewards (carrots) and punishments (sticks). This model worked in the early days of industrialization when tasks were simple and repetitive. Workers needed clear incentives to produce more goods, faster and cheaper. But as Pink points out, this system falters when applied to the complex, creative work of the modern world.

Motivation 2.0 doesn't just fail—it actively harms. It turns curiosity into compliance and passion into productivity. In school, I remember feeling a deep sense of wonder about the world, but there was never room for that in the classroom. The focus was always on the next test, the next grade, the next metric. Over time, that wonder began to fade, replaced by a sense of dread. What if I didn't measure up? What if I couldn't climb the tree?

Howard Gardner's theory of multiple intelligences offers an important critique of this system. Gardner argues that intelligence isn't a single, measurable entity but a diverse set of abilities—musical, interpersonal, spatial, and more. Motivation 2.0, however, doesn't account for this diversity. It treats everyone as though they should excel in the same ways, marginalizing those who think, learn, or create differently.

The Zoo: Controlled Freedom

If The Farm is a place of total control, The Zoo offers a kind of controlled freedom. At first glance, it seems like an improvement. The animals have more space to roam, more stimulation, more choices. But look closely, and you'll see the fences. The boundaries are invisible, but they're still there.

I've spent much of my adult life living in The Zoo. When I entered the workforce, I thought I'd escaped the constraints of school. I believed I was free to pursue my passions, to contribute in meaningful ways. But I quickly realized how limited that freedom was. My work wasn't about creativity or innovation—it was about meeting metrics, following rules, and staying within the lines. The Zoo offered safety and structure, but it came at the cost of autonomy.

This became especially clear when my health began to decline. The healthcare system, much like The Zoo, operates within a framework of controlled freedom. Doctors have protocols, insurance companies have guidelines, and patients are expected to fit into these predefined boxes. But what happens when you don't fit? When your symptoms don't align with the standard templates, you're dismissed, ignored, or worse—blamed for your own suffering.

I can't count how many times I was told, "Your tests are normal," as though that was the end of the conversation. My pain, my exhaustion, my dizziness—they were real, but they didn't fit into the system's metrics. I was pacing along the edges of the fence, searching for a way out, but the system wasn't designed to let me through.

The Consequences of Constraint

The consequences of Motivation 2.0 are far-reaching. In education, it stifles creativity and curiosity. In the workplace, it leads to burnout and disengagement. And in healthcare, it dehumanizes patients, reducing them to data points and diagnoses.

Albert Einstein's famous quote about the fish and the tree is more relevant than ever: "Everybody is a genius. But if you judge a fish by its ability to climb a tree, it will live its whole life believing it is stupid." Strive systems are built on this flawed logic. They measure success in narrow, standardized ways, ignoring the diversity of human potential.

But there is hope. As Pink points out, the limitations of Motivation 2.0 have led to the emergence of a new model: Motivation 3.0. This framework, built on autonomy, mastery, and purpose, offers a glimpse of what's possible when we move beyond the constraints of The Farm and The Zoo.

A Personal Reflection

When I think about The Farm and The Zoo, I think about the systems that have shaped my life. I think about the classrooms that asked me to fit a mold I was never meant to fit. I think about the workplaces that valued compliance over creativity. And I think about the doctors who couldn't see me as a person because I didn't fit into their templates.

But I also think about the moments when I glimpsed The Wild—when I felt free to explore, create, and connect in meaningful ways. These moments remind me that there's another way, a better way. The Wild isn't about chaos or anarchy. It's about balance. It's about creating systems that embrace abundance, interdependence, and resilience.

As we move forward, I want to invite you to reflect on the systems in your own life. Are you living in The Farm, The Zoo, or The Wild? And what would it take to create a world where all of us can thrive—not just survive or strive, but truly thrive?

Chapter 3: The Fish and the Tree

Albert Einstein once said, "Everybody is a genius. But if you judge a fish by its ability to climb a tree, it will live its whole life believing it is stupid." This quote has become a rallying cry for those of us who have felt out of place in systems that demand conformity. It's a reminder that our worth isn't defined by how well we fit into a single mold but by the unique qualities we bring to the table.

Yet, Strive systems—those rooted in control, scarcity, and standardization—operate on the assumption that there is only one path to success. They create metrics, benchmarks, and hierarchies that force us to climb the tree, regardless of whether we're fish, birds, or wolves. In the process, they dismiss the incredible diversity of human potential.

I know what it feels like to be the fish in the tree. For much of my life, I internalized the belief that my struggles were a personal failing rather than a reflection of a flawed system. I thought, *If I just try harder, I'll be able to make this work.* But no matter how hard I tried, I couldn't seem to meet the metrics. It wasn't until much later—after my ADHD diagnosis and self-recognition as autistic—that I began to see the bigger picture.

The Limits of Standardized Metrics

Howard Gardner's theory of multiple intelligences offers a powerful critique of Strive systems. Gardner argues that intelligence isn't a single, measurable entity but a diverse set of abilities: linguistic, logical-mathematical, spatial, musical, bodily-kinesthetic, interpersonal, intrapersonal, and naturalistic. Each of these intelligences reflects a different way of thinking, learning, and creating.

Yet, our education systems are designed to reward only a narrow slice of these intelligences. They prioritize linguistic and logical-mathematical abilities while marginalizing others. Music, art, and physical education are often treated as luxuries rather than essential parts of a well-rounded education. Students who excel in interpersonal or intrapersonal skills are rarely celebrated for their gifts. Instead, they are measured—and often found wanting—by standardized tests that favor conformity over creativity.

I remember sitting in classrooms as a child, feeling like I was being asked to solve a puzzle with missing pieces. The tests, the assignments, the expectations—they never seemed to align with the way my brain worked. I loved asking questions, exploring ideas, and making connections, but there was no metric for that. What mattered were the grades on my report card, the scores on my tests. And when those scores didn't measure up, I assumed the problem was me.

The same thing happened when I entered the workplace. Metrics like KPIs and performance reviews became the new report card. Once again, I found myself trying to climb a tree that I was never meant to climb. And once again, I internalized the belief that my struggles were a reflection of my own inadequacy.

The Cost of Marginalization

The cost of these Strive metrics isn't just personal—it's societal. By prioritizing standardization over individuality, we lose the incredible potential that comes from diverse ways of thinking. Gardner's theory of multiple intelligences isn't just a critique of education; it's a call to action. It asks us to create systems that celebrate, rather than constrain, human diversity.

Einstein's metaphor of the fish and the tree is a perfect illustration of this. It's not just the fish that suffers when it's judged by its ability to climb—the entire ecosystem suffers. In a healthy ecosystem, every organism plays a role. The fish doesn't need to climb the tree because it has its own unique niche. It contributes to the health of the ecosystem in ways that no other organism can.

The same is true of human systems. When we marginalize those who don't fit the mold, we lose out on their unique contributions. This is especially true for neurodivergent individuals, whose ways of thinking and problem-solving often fall outside the bounds of traditional metrics.

A Personal Reflection

When I reflect on my own experiences, I think about how much of my potential was overlooked or dismissed by systems that weren't designed to see it. I think about the teachers who encouraged me to conform rather than celebrate my creativity. I think about the workplaces that valued efficiency over innovation. And I think about the healthcare professionals who dismissed my symptoms because they didn't fit into their templates.

But I also think about the moments when someone did see me—when they recognized and valued my unique abilities. One of those moments came from a friend who told me, "The way you see the world is something special." At the time, I didn't believe it. I was too caught up in the metrics, too focused on the ways I felt like I was falling short. But their words stayed with me, slowly shifting the way I saw myself.

This is why I believe so deeply in the principles of Thrive. Thrive systems recognize that success isn't about fitting into a single mold—it's about finding your own path, your own niche, and contributing in ways that are uniquely yours.

The Fish in the Wild

The Wild offers a powerful contrast to the constraints of The Farm and The Zoo. In the Wild, there are no standardized metrics. There's no single definition of success. Instead, the focus is on balance, diversity, and interdependence. Every organism has a role to play, and every role is valued.

In human terms, this means creating systems that celebrate multiple intelligences, diverse perspectives, and unique ways of thinking. It means moving beyond standardized tests and KPIs to embrace a broader, more inclusive definition of success. It means recognizing that thriving isn't about climbing the tree—it's about finding your place in the ecosystem.

As we continue this journey, I invite you to reflect on your own experiences with Strive metrics. Where have you felt like the fish in the tree? And what would it look like to create a world where every fish, every bird, every wolf has the freedom to thrive?

Chapter 4: Why Drive Alone Isn't Enough

Daniel Pink's *Drive* introduced us to a groundbreaking framework for understanding human motivation. Built on the principles of autonomy, mastery, and purpose, Motivation 3.0 is a powerful critique of the carrot-and-stick model that has dominated for centuries. Pink argues that when people are given the freedom to choose their path, the opportunity to develop their skills, and a sense of meaning in their work, they thrive. And yet, despite the transformative potential of these ideas, there's a critical challenge: Motivation 3.0 operates within systems that are still fundamentally built on scarcity and control.

This is the paradox we face today. While individuals may achieve autonomy, mastery, and purpose in their own lives, they remain constrained by larger systems that operate on outdated principles. It's like planting a wildflower in a concrete garden—no matter how resilient the flower is, it's limited by the environment around it.

The Hardware Problem

To understand why Drive alone isn't enough, we need to look at what Michel Foucault described as the "technologies of power." Foucault argued that systems of control—whether in education, healthcare, or the workplace—are not just external forces but deeply embedded structures that shape how we think, act, and relate to one another. These systems are the hardware of society, and they determine the limits of what is possible.

Take the workplace as an example. Pink's principles of Motivation 3.0 have been embraced by companies like Google and Netflix, which offer employees greater autonomy and encourage innovation. But even in these forward-thinking organizations, workers are still subject to the pressures of quarterly earnings reports, market competition, and shareholder expectations. The hardware of the system remains the same, even if the software has been upgraded.

I've experienced this tension firsthand. When I was working in a traditional office environment, I often found myself torn between the desire to do meaningful work and the need to meet arbitrary deadlines and performance metrics. No matter how much autonomy I was given in my day-to-day tasks, I couldn't escape the larger forces that prioritized efficiency over creativity, compliance over connection.

The Illusion of Freedom

Howard Gardner's critique of modern education offers a similar lens. Gardner's theory of multiple intelligences challenges the idea that there is one "correct" way to learn or succeed. And yet, even in schools that adopt more progressive approaches—like project-based learning or individualized instruction—the underlying system often remains the same. Students are still judged by standardized tests, still funneled into predefined career paths, still told to measure their worth by their output.

This illusion of freedom is what makes Motivation 3.0 so appealing yet so incomplete. It promises a better way to live and work, but it doesn't address the larger systemic barriers that limit our potential. As Foucault reminds us, true freedom requires not just a change in behavior but a transformation of the systems themselves.

Aldo Leopold captured this idea beautifully when he wrote, "Harmony with land is like harmony with a friend; you cannot cherish his right hand and chop off his left." The same is true of our systems. We cannot achieve harmony—true thriving—if we cling to systems that are fundamentally out of balance.

The Cost of Conformity

The cost of these imbalanced systems is felt most acutely by those who don't fit the mold. As someone who identifies as neurodivergent, I've often found myself at odds with systems that demand conformity. Whether it's the workplace, the classroom, or the doctor's office, the message is always the same: *Fit the mold or be left behind.*

This is the experience of many marginalized groups—not just neurodivergent individuals, but also those with chronic illnesses, disabilities, or unconventional ways of thinking. As Viktor Frankl wrote in *Man's Search for Meaning*, "Everything can be taken from a man but one thing: the last of the human freedoms—to choose one's attitude in any given set of circumstances." Yet, for so many of us, even this freedom feels like a distant dream when we are trapped in systems that stifle our potential.

When I was navigating the healthcare system, struggling to find answers for my symptoms of EDS and POTS, I felt this stifling firsthand. Every interaction was shaped by a system that prioritized speed over care, efficiency over empathy. It didn't matter that I was asking the right questions or advocating for myself. The system wasn't designed to see me as a person—it was designed to see me as a problem to solve, or worse, a problem to ignore.

A Glimpse of the Wild

Despite these challenges, there are moments when we catch glimpses of what is possible—moments when the constraints of Strive systems fall away, and we experience the freedom and abundance of the Wild. These moments often come when we connect with others in meaningful ways, when we find communities that value our unique perspectives, or when we have the courage to create something new.

In my own life, one of these moments came when I began to embrace my neurodivergence not as a limitation but as a strength. I started to see how my way of thinking—my need for autonomy, my resistance to arbitrary rules—could be a source of creativity and innovation. And I began to imagine what it would look like to build systems that didn't just tolerate diversity but actively celebrated it.

Pink's framework of autonomy, mastery, and purpose offers a powerful starting point for this vision. But to truly thrive, we need to go further. We need to redesign the hardware of our systems, creating environments that prioritize abundance, interdependence, and resilience.

The Promise of Thrive

This is the promise of Thrive: a world where individuals are not just free to pursue their own potential but supported by systems that amplify their creativity, their curiosity, and their connection to others. It's a world where we don't just upgrade the software but transform the hardware itself.

As we move forward, I invite you to reflect on the systems in your own life. Where have you experienced the limits of Motivation 3.0? And what would it take to create a world where Drive isn't the end of the journey, but the beginning of something much greater?

Chapter 5: Strive Under Fear – Control, Conformity, and Subversion

Fear is one of the most potent forces that drive human behavior. Throughout history, systems built on control and scarcity have wielded fear as a tool to enforce conformity, suppress dissent, and maintain power. These are the hallmark traits of what I call **Strive systems**—systems that thrive not on innovation or collaboration but on control and compliance.

Michel Foucault described this phenomenon as *biopower*, a mechanism by which systems regulate our bodies and lives. Through surveillance, discipline, and normalization, biopower ensures that we stay within the bounds of what is deemed acceptable. And when fear is weaponized—whether through laws, cultural norms, or social stigmas—it becomes a powerful tool for silencing those who dare to question the system.

McCarthyism and the Lavender Scare

The era of McCarthyism offers a stark example of fear-driven systems at their most extreme. In the 1950s, Senator Joseph McCarthy led a campaign to root out alleged communists from American institutions. But this crusade wasn't limited to political ideology—it extended into the personal lives of citizens. The **Lavender Scare**, a parallel effort to purge LGBTQ+ individuals from government positions, revealed the insidious ways fear and conformity intersect.

As Foucault would argue, these efforts were about more than political control; they were about shaping the very fabric of society. LGBTQ+ individuals were labeled as moral subversives, their identities framed as threats to national security. This wasn't just about silencing dissent—it was about enforcing a narrow definition of what it meant to belong.

Reading about these moments in history, I couldn't help but think about how fear operates in modern systems. While the Lavender Scare may seem like a relic of the past, its echoes are still felt today. Fear of difference, fear of scarcity, and fear of change continue to shape how we treat those who don't fit the mold.

The Personal Cost of Fear-Driven Systems

For me, the cost of fear-driven systems has been deeply personal. As someone who identifies as neurodivergent, I've often felt the pressure to conform to expectations that don't align with who I am. Whether it was in school, where standardized tests measured my worth, or in the workplace, where rigid hierarchies dictated my value, the message was always the same: *Fit the mold or be left behind.*

This pressure to conform isn't unique to me. It's a reality for anyone who exists outside the "norm." Women with chronic illnesses, for example, are often dismissed as hysterical when their symptoms don't fit neatly into medical templates. Neurodivergent individuals are labeled as "difficult" or "uncooperative" when they resist arbitrary rules. And those who challenge systemic injustice are branded as troublemakers, their voices silenced by fear and conformity.

Viktor Frankl wrote in *Man's Search for Meaning*, "Everything can be taken from a man but one thing: the last of the human freedoms—to choose one's attitude in any given set of circumstances." Yet, in fear-driven systems, even this freedom feels tenuous. When fear dictates our choices, it becomes nearly impossible to imagine alternatives—to see beyond the constraints of the system.

Control vs. Creativity

The problem with fear-driven systems is that they prioritize control over creativity. Howard Gardner's work on multiple intelligences shows us the incredible diversity of human potential, but fear stifles that potential. It tells us to stay in our lane, to avoid rocking the boat, to meet the metrics and nothing more.

This was my experience in the healthcare system. As I sought answers for my symptoms of EDS and POTS, I encountered doctors who seemed more interested in controlling the narrative than listening to my story. They relied on protocols and checklists, dismissing anything that fell outside their narrow scope of understanding. It wasn't just frustrating—it was dehumanizing.

This need for control extends beyond healthcare. In education, it's the standardization of success that leaves so many students behind. In the workplace, it's the rigid hierarchies that stifle innovation. And in society, it's the fear of difference that marginalizes those who don't conform.

The Courage to Subvert

But even in the face of fear, there have always been those who dare to subvert the system. LGBTQ+ activists during the Lavender Scare, for example, refused to disappear quietly. They organized, resisted, and laid the groundwork for the modern LGBTQ+ rights movement. Their courage reminds us that change is possible—even in the most fear-driven systems.

This courage to subvert is what inspires me when I think about the principles of **Thrive**. Thrive systems are not about control—they're about trust. They recognize that creativity, connection, and diversity are not threats but strengths. They create spaces where people are free to question, explore, and innovate without fear of punishment.

In my own life, I've found glimpses of Thrive in unexpected places. I think about the online communities of people with POTS and EDS who have challenged the stereotypes and misinformation that dominate the medical field. Through their collective efforts, they've begun to hold the system accountable, forcing it to confront its flaws. It's a small but powerful example of what happens when we move beyond fear and toward resilience.

A Glimpse of the Wild

The Wild offers a compelling alternative to fear-driven systems. In the Wild, there is no need for control or conformity because the system itself is balanced. Diversity is not just tolerated—it's essential. Every organism has a role to play, and every role is valued.

In human terms, this means creating systems that embrace abundance, interdependence, and resilience. It means moving beyond fear and scarcity to build communities where everyone has the freedom to contribute in meaningful ways.

As we continue this journey, I invite you to reflect on the role of fear in your own life. Where have you felt its constraints? And what would it take to create a world where courage—not fear—is the foundation of our systems?

Chapter 6: Pathological Demand Avoidance and the Pariah Problem

For those who resist conformity, Strive systems often feel like a trap. These systems, designed to reward obedience and punish deviation, leave little room for individuals whose autonomy and creativity make them fundamentally unsuited to compliance. The result is a phenomenon I call the **Pariah Problem**—the alienation and marginalization of individuals who cannot or will not fit into the molds these systems create.

As someone with a PDA (Pathological Demand Avoidance) profile of autism, I've lived this reality firsthand. PDA is characterized by an intense need for autonomy and an equally intense resistance to demands, even when they're self-imposed. For much of my life, I thought this resistance was a flaw—a sign that I wasn't trying hard enough, wasn't disciplined enough, wasn't "normal" enough. But the more I've learned about PDA, the more I've realized that my resistance isn't the problem. The problem is the system.

The Demand for Compliance

Judith Butler's theory of performativity offers a powerful lens through which to view the Pariah Problem. Butler argues that societal norms are not natural or inevitable; they are performances that we are taught to enact. When we fail to perform these roles correctly—whether by resisting authority, questioning norms, or simply existing outside the boundaries of what is deemed "acceptable"—we are punished, excluded, or erased.

In education, this manifests as the student who refuses to follow the rules and is labeled a troublemaker. In the workplace, it's the employee who challenges the status quo and is sidelined or fired. In healthcare, it's the patient whose symptoms don't fit the textbook and is dismissed as hysterical or malingering. Strive systems demand compliance, and those who resist are cast as pariahs.

I've felt this in countless ways. As a child, I was constantly told to "just follow the rules," but rules that seemed arbitrary or unfair filled me with a visceral sense of resistance. In the workplace, I struggled to fit into hierarchies that prioritized obedience over innovation. And in the healthcare system, my refusal to accept dismissive diagnoses often led to more frustration than answers.

The Creativity of Resistance

What Strive systems fail to recognize is that resistance is often a form of creativity. When we push back against demands that feel wrong or limiting, we are not just rejecting the status quo—we are imagining alternatives. Michel Foucault argued that power and resistance are inherently linked; wherever there is power, there is also the possibility of resistance. This resistance is not a flaw—it is a source of strength.

Think about some of the most transformative figures in history: artists, scientists, activists. Their resistance to the systems of their time wasn't a failure to conform—it was a refusal to accept constraints on their vision. Albert Einstein, who famously declared that "imagination is more important than knowledge," was known for his disdain for authority and his refusal to follow conventional paths. His resistance wasn't just an act of defiance—it was an act of creation.

For me, this realization has been deeply liberating. What I once saw as a defect—my inability to comply with arbitrary demands—I now see as a strength. My resistance has forced me to think critically about the systems I live in and to imagine better ways of being. It has taught me to value autonomy, creativity, and integrity over conformity and convenience.

The Cost of Marginalization

But this resistance comes at a cost. Strive systems are not kind to those who refuse to comply. They label us as difficult, disruptive, or uncooperative. They exclude us from opportunities, deny us resources, and punish us for our defiance.

This is particularly true for neurodivergent individuals, whose needs and strengths often fall outside the boundaries of what Strive systems are designed to accommodate. The rise of awareness around ADHD and autism has brought some progress, but many of these conversations are still framed in terms of deficits rather than differences. We are seen as problems to be solved rather than people to be understood.

For women, this marginalization is compounded by societal norms that label them as hysterical or overly emotional when they advocate for themselves. In healthcare, women with chronic illnesses like EDS and POTS are often dismissed or misdiagnosed because their symptoms don't fit neatly into medical templates. These patterns of exclusion are not random—they are the logical outcome of systems that value compliance over complexity.

Thrive and the Pariah Problem

The principles of Thrive offer a powerful alternative to the Pariah Problem. Where Strive systems demand compliance, Thrive systems celebrate autonomy. Where Strive systems punish deviation, Thrive systems recognize resistance as a source of creativity. And where Strive systems marginalize those who don't fit, Thrive systems create spaces where everyone has the freedom to contribute in ways that are uniquely theirs.

This shift requires a fundamental rethinking of how we design our systems. It means creating education systems that value curiosity over compliance, workplaces that prioritize collaboration over hierarchy, and healthcare systems that see patients as partners rather than problems.

In my own life, I've found glimpses of Thrive in the communities I've built and the people who have supported me. These are the spaces where I've been free to be myself—where my resistance has been seen not as defiance but as a form of creativity. These moments remind me that Thrive isn't just a concept—it's a possibility. And it's one we can all work toward.

A Reflection on Resistance

As I write this, I think about how much of my life has been shaped by resistance. I think about the rules I refused to follow, the hierarchies I refused to accept, the systems I refused to trust. And I think about how much strength I've found in that resistance—how it has forced me to think critically, act boldly, and imagine a world beyond the constraints of Strive.

But I also think about the cost of that resistance. The jobs I've lost, the opportunities I've missed, the relationships I've strained. Resistance is not easy, and it is not always rewarded. But it is necessary. As Judith Butler reminds us, "The task is not whether to resist, but how to resist, and how to organize resistance in ways that generate the least suffering."

This is the promise of Thrive: a world where resistance is not punished but celebrated. A world where those of us who have been cast as pariahs can find our place—not by conforming, but by being ourselves.

Chapter 7: The Cost of Strive

Strive systems, with their emphasis on control, scarcity, and standardized metrics, are often upheld as necessary frameworks for progress. Yet, beneath their promises of stability and efficiency lies a profound cost—a cost paid not only by individuals but also by society as a whole. These systems, built to optimize productivity, often do so at the expense of creativity, connection, and well-being.

For me, the cost of Strive has been deeply personal. As someone who has navigated both the workplace and the healthcare system with neurodivergence and chronic illness, I've experienced firsthand how these systems fail those who don't fit their molds. They ask us to give everything we have to meet their demands, only to abandon us when we can no longer keep up.

The Psychological Toll

The psychological toll of Strive systems is immense. Viktor Frankl, in *Man's Search for Meaning*, wrote, "What is to give light must endure burning." While this sentiment speaks to the resilience of the human spirit, it also highlights the danger of systems that burn individuals out without offering them a path to renewal. Strive systems demand constant output but rarely provide the support needed to sustain it.

In education, this manifests as students who internalize the belief that their worth is tied to their grades and test scores. In the workplace, it's employees who feel trapped in cycles of overwork and burnout, afraid to take risks for fear of failure. And in healthcare, it's patients who are dismissed or blamed for their conditions, left to navigate a system that sees them as problems to be solved rather than people to be cared for.

I remember the deep sense of inadequacy I felt when I could no longer meet the demands of the systems I once thrived in. My health was deteriorating, and every attempt to seek help seemed to end in frustration. Doctors told me my symptoms didn't fit their frameworks, and employers saw my struggles as a lack of commitment rather than a sign that I needed support. The system wasn't built to see me as a whole person—it was built to extract as much as it could from me, then move on.

The Social Cost

The cost of Strive extends beyond the individual. By prioritizing efficiency and competition, these systems erode the very foundations of community and collaboration. Aldo Leopold once observed, "We abuse the land because we regard it as a commodity belonging to us." The same can be said of how we treat one another in Strive systems. When people are reduced to their utility—what they can produce or achieve—we lose sight of their humanity.

This commodification of people is particularly evident in economic systems that thrive on scarcity. Kate Raworth, in her book *Doughnut Economics*, critiques the obsession with GDP growth as a measure of success. She argues that this focus on endless growth not only harms the planet but also perpetuates inequality and disconnection. Strive systems create a zero-sum game, where the success of one often comes at the expense of another.

I've felt this disconnection most acutely in the healthcare system. As someone with Ehlers-Danlos Syndrome (EDS) and Postural Orthostatic Tachycardia Syndrome (POTS), I've seen how financial incentives and rigid protocols can overshadow patient care. When profit becomes the priority, the humanity of the system is lost. The result is a system that leaves people like me feeling invisible, unheard, and unsupported.

The Creativity Deficit

Strive systems also come at a cost to creativity and innovation. Howard Gardner's theory of multiple intelligences reminds us of the incredible diversity of human potential. Yet, when systems prioritize standardized metrics over individual strengths, they stifle the very qualities that drive progress.

Albert Einstein famously said, "Imagination is more important than knowledge." But in Strive systems, imagination is often seen as a luxury rather than a necessity. Students are taught to memorize rather than question, employees are rewarded for compliance rather than innovation, and patients are expected to follow protocols rather than advocate for their unique needs.

As someone who has always thrived on curiosity and creativity, I've struggled to navigate systems that value efficiency over exploration. Whether it was in school, where I felt constrained by rigid curricula, or in the workplace, where my ideas were often dismissed as impractical, I've seen how these systems fail to nurture the very qualities that make us human.

The Cost of Disconnection

At its core, the greatest cost of Strive systems is disconnection. By framing life as a competition, these systems pit us against one another rather than encouraging us to work together. They create silos, separating individuals from their communities and even from themselves.

Brené Brown, in her research on vulnerability and connection, reminds us that "we are wired for connection." Yet, Strive systems often make genuine connection feel impossible. In my own life, I've experienced this disconnection in countless ways. When my health began to decline, I felt isolated—not just from the systems that were supposed to support me, but from the people around me. It wasn't until I found online communities of individuals with POTS and EDS that I began to feel a sense of belonging again.

These communities, built on mutual support and shared experiences, showed me what was possible when we move beyond the competitive, scarcity-driven mindset of Strive. They reminded me that connection isn't just a nice-to-have—it's essential for resilience and growth.

A Reflection on Cost

As I reflect on the cost of Strive, I think about the countless individuals who have been left behind by systems that prioritize efficiency over humanity. I think about the students who are told they'll never succeed because they don't fit the mold. I think about the employees who burn out because they're afraid to take a break. And I think about the patients who are dismissed because their symptoms don't fit the template.

But I also think about the moments when I've glimpsed what's possible—when I've seen the power of connection, creativity, and community. These moments remind me that the cost of Strive isn't inevitable. It's a choice. And it's one we can choose to change.

A Glimpse of Thrive

Thrive systems offer a powerful alternative to the disconnection of Strive. They recognize that progress isn't about competition—it's about collaboration. They value creativity, not as a luxury but as a necessity. And they prioritize connection, creating environments where everyone has the freedom to contribute in meaningful ways.

As we continue this journey, I invite you to reflect on the cost of Strive in your own life. Where have you felt its constraints? And what would it take to create a world where connection, creativity, and community are not the exceptions but the norm?

Chapter 8: The Principles of Thrive

If Strive systems are built on control, scarcity, and standardization, Thrive systems offer a transformative alternative. Thrive is not just about personal success or individual resilience—it's about creating environments where everyone has the freedom to flourish. At its core, Thrive is built on three guiding principles: **Abundance, Interdependence, and Resilience**. These principles are not just theoretical—they are deeply human values rooted in our history, our biology, and our aspirations for the future.

Abundance: Moving Beyond Scarcity

Strive systems operate on the assumption of scarcity: there is never enough time, money, or resources, and success is a zero-sum game. This scarcity mindset creates competition, fear, and hoarding—whether it's in economics, education, or healthcare. Thrive systems, by contrast, are rooted in the principle of **abundance**: the belief that collaboration and shared resources create more opportunities for everyone.

Kate Raworth, in her groundbreaking work *Doughnut Economics*, critiques the obsession with endless growth as both unsustainable and unnecessary. She argues that the true measure of progress isn't GDP but whether humanity can meet its needs within the planet's ecological limits. Thrive systems embrace this perspective, prioritizing sustainability and cooperation over competition and extraction.

I've seen the power of abundance in unexpected places. When I first connected with online communities of individuals with POTS and EDS, I was struck by how freely people shared their experiences, resources, and advice. There was no competition—just a collective commitment to helping one another. These communities showed me that abundance isn't about having infinite resources—it's about recognizing that when we share what we have, we all benefit.

Albert Einstein once said, "Only a life lived for others is a life worthwhile." This captures the essence of abundance. Thrive systems challenge us to move beyond the scarcity mindset and imagine a world where collaboration, not competition, is the foundation of progress.

Interdependence: The Strength of Connection

The second principle of Thrive is **interdependence**—the recognition that no one thrives alone. Just as ecosystems rely on the diversity and cooperation of their members, human systems flourish when they embrace connection and collaboration.

Elinor Ostrom's research on the commons offers a compelling model for interdependence. Ostrom demonstrated that communities can sustainably manage shared resources—like fisheries, forests, and irrigation systems—when they prioritize trust, communication, and shared responsibility. Her work challenges the idea that competition is the only path to progress, showing instead that cooperation is not only possible but essential.

In my own life, interdependence has often felt like both a challenge and a gift. As someone who values autonomy, I've struggled to ask for help when I've needed it most. But during some of my darkest moments—when my health was failing, and the systems I relied on were letting me down—it was the support of others that kept me going.

I think about my friend Brian Stearns, who stepped in when I felt invisible and overwhelmed. His belief in me reminded me of the words of Les Brown:

"Other people's opinions of you do not have to become your reality." Brian's unwavering support helped me see beyond the constraints of Strive systems, reminding me that interdependence isn't a weakness—it's a strength.

Brené Brown, in her research on vulnerability and connection, writes, "Connection is why we're here; it is what gives purpose and meaning to our lives." Thrive systems embrace this truth, creating environments where connection is not just encouraged but celebrated.

Resilience: Thriving Through Change

The third principle of Thrive is **resilience**—the ability to adapt, grow, and thrive in the face of change and adversity. Resilience is not just about bouncing back—it's about learning from challenges and emerging stronger.

Viktor Frankl's *Man's Search for Meaning* offers a powerful exploration of resilience. Frankl, who survived the horrors of the Holocaust, wrote that "when we are no longer able to change a situation, we are challenged to change ourselves." This ability to find meaning in suffering, to adapt to circumstances beyond our control, is at the heart of resilience.

In the natural world, resilience is everywhere. Forests recover from fires, ecosystems adapt to changing climates, and species evolve in response to new challenges. Thrive systems take inspiration from this resilience, designing environments that are flexible, adaptive, and supportive.

For me, resilience has been a constant theme in my journey with chronic illness and neurodivergence. I've had to learn how to adapt to systems that weren't designed for me, to advocate for myself when no one else would, and to find meaning in experiences that often felt overwhelming. Resilience hasn't always come easily, but it has taught me that thriving isn't about avoiding challenges—it's about growing through them.

The Promise of Thrive

Abundance, interdependence, and resilience are not just abstract ideals—they are principles that can transform how we live, work, and connect. Thrive systems challenge us to move beyond the limitations of Strive, creating environments where everyone has the freedom to flourish.

In education, this means moving away from standardized tests and embracing curiosity-driven learning. Howard Gardner's theory of multiple intelligences offers a powerful framework for this shift, showing us that students thrive when their unique strengths are recognized and nurtured.

In healthcare, it means treating patients as partners rather than problems. It means listening to their stories, valuing their experiences, and designing systems that prioritize care over efficiency.

In the workplace, it means creating cultures of trust and innovation, where failure is seen not as a setback but as a stepping stone to growth. As Brené Brown reminds us, "Vulnerability is the birthplace of innovation, creativity, and change."

A Reflection on Principles

As I reflect on these principles, I think about how much they've shaped my own journey. Abundance has taught me the power of sharing, interdependence has shown me the strength of connection, and resilience has reminded me that thriving isn't about perfection—it's about growth.

But I also think about the work that remains. Thrive isn't just a personal practice—it's a collective challenge. It asks us to reimagine the systems that shape our lives, to move beyond the constraints of Strive, and to build a world where flourishing is possible for everyone.

So I leave you with this question: What would it look like to create a world rooted in abundance, interdependence, and resilience? And what role will you play in making that world a reality?

Chapter 9: Rewilding Education

Education is the foundation of every society. It shapes not only what we know but also how we think, solve problems, and engage with the world. Yet, for all its potential, our current education system operates largely within the constraints of **Strive systems**. It prioritizes standardization, efficiency, and control over creativity, curiosity, and connection. To create a world where we truly thrive, we must reimagine education—not as a system of compliance, but as a space of exploration and growth. We must rewild it.

The Constraints of Standardization

Our education system was designed during the Industrial Revolution to meet the needs of a factory-driven economy. Students were treated as raw materials to be shaped into productive workers, and success was measured by standardized metrics: test scores, grades, and graduation rates. While this system served its purpose in a time of rapid industrialization, it is woefully inadequate for the complexities of the modern world.

Howard Gardner's theory of multiple intelligences exposes the limitations of this approach. Gardner argues that intelligence is not a single, measurable entity but a rich tapestry of abilities, including linguistic, logical-mathematical, musical, spatial, bodily-kinesthetic, interpersonal, intrapersonal, and naturalistic intelligences. Yet, our schools prioritize only a narrow subset of these abilities, leaving countless students feeling marginalized and inadequate.

I know this feeling well. As a student, I often struggled to conform to the expectations of a system that valued rote memorization and rigid compliance over curiosity and creativity. I loved asking questions, exploring ideas, and making connections, but there was no metric for that. What mattered were my test scores and my ability to follow instructions. And when I fell short of those metrics, I assumed the problem was me.

Albert Einstein famously said, "Education is what remains after one has forgotten what one has learned in school." This sentiment captures the disconnect between what education could be—a tool for discovery and growth—and what it often is: a system of control that prioritizes conformity over curiosity.

The Zoo of Controlled Learning

Even in schools that adopt more progressive approaches, the underlying system often remains unchanged. Project-based learning, individualized instruction, and creativity-driven curricula are steps in the right direction, but they often exist within the constraints of standardized tests and predefined outcomes. These schools operate within what I call the **Zoo of Controlled Learning**: environments that simulate freedom but still prioritize control.

Michel Foucault's concept of "disciplinary power" is especially relevant here. Foucault argued that modern institutions, including schools, use subtle forms of control to shape behavior and enforce norms. In the Zoo of Controlled Learning, students may have more choices, but those choices are often limited by the boundaries of the system. True freedom—the kind that allows for exploration, failure, and growth—remains elusive.

I've seen this dynamic play out in my own life. When I returned to education as an adult, I hoped to find a system that valued my unique perspective and way of thinking. Instead, I encountered the same constraints I had faced as a child: rigid curricula, narrow definitions of success, and little room for creativity. It wasn't until I began exploring alternative approaches, like self-directed learning and project-based education, that I began to see what was possible.

The Wild: A New Vision for Education

Rewilding education means moving beyond the constraints of the farm and the zoo to create environments that embrace the principles of abundance, interdependence, and resilience. It means recognizing that learning is not a linear process but a dynamic, interconnected journey.

Paulo Freire's *Pedagogy of the Oppressed* offers a powerful framework for this transformation. Freire argued that traditional education, which he called the "banking model," treats students as empty vessels to be filled with knowledge. This approach, he believed, reinforces systems of oppression by denying students the opportunity to think critically and engage with the world on their own terms. Instead, Freire advocated for a "problem-posing" model of education, where students and teachers collaborate to explore questions, challenge assumptions, and co-create knowledge.

Montessori and Waldorf schools provide real-world examples of this vision. These models prioritize curiosity, creativity, and holistic development over standardized outcomes. Students are encouraged to follow their interests, learn at their own pace, and develop skills that align with their unique strengths and passions. While these approaches are often seen as niche or alternative, they offer valuable insights into what education could look like in a Thrive system.

A Personal Reflection

Rewilding education is deeply personal for me. As someone who has struggled to fit into traditional systems, I've often felt like the fish in Einstein's metaphor, judged by my ability to climb a tree. But I've also glimpsed what's possible when education embraces the Wild—when students are free to explore, fail, and grow in ways that align with their unique abilities.

One of the most transformative moments in my own learning journey came when I discovered project-based education. For the first time, I was encouraged to pursue questions that mattered to me, to think critically about the world, and to connect my learning to real-world challenges. This experience showed me that education doesn't have to be about compliance—it can be about discovery, growth, and connection.

But I also think about the countless students who never have the chance to experience this kind of learning. I think about the children who are labeled as troublemakers or failures because they don't fit into the system's narrow definitions of success. And I think about the educators who are forced to prioritize test scores over the well-being and growth of their students.

The Promise of Rewilding

Rewilding education is not just about improving individual outcomes—it's about transforming the systems that shape our lives. It's about creating environments where students can thrive, not just survive. It's about moving beyond standardized metrics to embrace the full spectrum of human potential.

As we continue this journey, I invite you to reflect on your own experiences with education. Where have you felt constrained by the system? And what would it look like to create a world where learning is not a means to an end, but an end in itself?

Chapter 10: Rewilding the Economy

Economies are the lifeblood of societies, shaping how resources are distributed, how opportunities are created, and how value is measured. But like our education systems, modern economies are trapped in Strive frameworks that prioritize scarcity, competition, and control. They are built on outdated assumptions that no longer serve the needs of people or the planet. To move from Strive to Thrive, we must reimagine our economies—not as systems of extraction and scarcity, but as ecosystems of abundance, interdependence, and resilience.

The Scarcity Mindset

At the heart of our economic systems lies the scarcity mindset: the belief that resources are finite and must be fought over, hoarded, and controlled. This mindset is embedded in everything from corporate strategies to government policies. It drives inequality, fuels environmental destruction, and creates a culture of competition that pits individuals and communities against one another.

Kate Raworth, in her book *Doughnut Economics*, critiques this mindset and offers a compelling alternative. She argues that economies should be designed to meet the needs of all people while respecting the ecological boundaries of the planet. Her model, shaped like a doughnut, emphasizes the balance between a social foundation that ensures everyone has access to basic needs and an ecological ceiling that prevents environmental degradation.

I've often felt the weight of the scarcity mindset in my own life. Growing up, I internalized the idea that success meant outcompeting others—whether it was for grades, jobs, or resources. But as I've navigated the challenges of chronic illness and neurodivergence, I've come to see how limiting this mindset truly is. The more I focused on scarcity, the more isolated and disconnected I felt. It wasn't until I began exploring alternative economic models—like mutual aid networks and community-driven initiatives—that I began to see the possibilities of abundance.

The Problem of Growth

Another hallmark of Strive economies is their obsession with growth. Gross Domestic Product (GDP) has long been the primary measure of economic success, but it tells us little about the well-being of people or the health of the planet. As Robert F. Kennedy famously said, "GDP measures everything except that which makes life worthwhile."

This obsession with growth has profound consequences. It drives environmental destruction as industries extract resources at unsustainable rates. It exacerbates inequality, as wealth accumulates at the top while others are left behind. And it perpetuates a culture of endless striving, where the pursuit of more is valued over the quality of life.

Elinor Ostrom's work on the commons offers a powerful critique of growth-centric models. Ostrom demonstrated that communities can sustainably manage shared resources through cooperation, trust, and shared responsibility. Her research challenges the notion that private ownership and competition are the only paths to economic success, showing instead that collaboration and stewardship can create more sustainable and equitable outcomes.

The Zoo of Managed Economies

Even when economies attempt to address issues like inequality and environmental degradation, they often do so within the constraints of Strive systems. Policies are designed to manage scarcity rather than challenge it. Initiatives focus on redistribution rather than reimagination. These are the hallmarks of what I call the **Zoo of Managed Economies**: systems that simulate abundance but remain fundamentally rooted in control and scarcity.

I've seen the limitations of managed economies in my own life. As someone who has relied on social safety nets during periods of financial instability, I've experienced both their necessity and their shortcomings. While these systems provide essential support, they often come with layers of bureaucracy and restrictions that make it difficult to truly thrive. They offer just enough to survive but rarely enough to escape the cycle of scarcity.

The Wild: A New Vision for Economies

Rewilding the economy means moving beyond the constraints of the farm and the zoo to create systems that embrace abundance, interdependence, and resilience. It means designing economies that prioritize well-being over growth, collaboration over competition, and sustainability over extraction.

Raworth's *Doughnut Economics* provides a powerful framework for this vision. By focusing on the balance between social and ecological needs, her model challenges us to rethink what economic success looks like. Instead of measuring progress by GDP, we can measure it by the health of our communities, the sustainability of our practices, and the opportunities we create for future generations.

In practice, this could mean expanding universal basic income (UBI) programs, as seen in Finland's pilot project, where participants reported lower stress and greater freedom to pursue education and entrepreneurship. It could mean investing in regenerative agriculture, which restores ecosystems while producing food. And it could mean embracing cooperative business models that prioritize shared ownership and decision-making.

A Personal Reflection

Rewilding the economy is not just an abstract ideal for me—it's deeply personal. As someone who has struggled to navigate traditional economic systems, I've felt the weight of scarcity, the pressure of competition, and the limitations of managed support. But I've also glimpsed the possibilities of abundance through community-driven initiatives and collaborative efforts.

One of the most transformative experiences for me was participating in a mutual aid network during a particularly difficult period in my life. This network wasn't about charity—it was about solidarity. People came together to share resources, skills, and support, creating a microcosm of what a rewilded economy could look like. It wasn't perfect, but it was a powerful reminder that abundance is possible when we prioritize connection and collaboration.

Brené Brown writes, "We don't have to do all of it alone. We were never meant to." This truth lies at the heart of rewilding the economy. It's about recognizing that no one thrives in isolation and that our greatest strength comes from working together.

The Promise of Rewilding

Rewilding the economy is not just a response to the failures of Strive systems—it's a vision for a better future. It challenges us to move beyond the scarcity mindset and embrace the principles of abundance, interdependence, and resilience. It asks us to reimagine what progress looks like and to design systems that prioritize well-being, sustainability, and connection.

As we continue this journey, I invite you to reflect on your own experiences with the economy. Where have you felt the constraints of scarcity? And what would it look like to create a world where the economy isn't a source of stress but a foundation for flourishing?

Chapter 11: Breaking Free of Strive Metrics

In Strive systems, metrics are the ultimate measure of success. They are the benchmarks that determine whether we've succeeded or failed, whether we're worthy or wanting. From grades in school to performance reviews at work, these metrics shape how we see ourselves and how society values us. But what if these metrics are fundamentally flawed? What if, by focusing so narrowly on measurable outcomes, we're missing what truly matters?

Breaking free of Strive metrics isn't just about rejecting old standards—it's about redefining success in ways that align with the principles of Thrive: **abundance, interdependence, and resilience**.

The Tyranny of Metrics

The tyranny of metrics is a hallmark of Strive systems. These metrics reduce complex human experiences to simple numbers, stripping away nuance and context. In education, standardized tests measure intelligence and potential in narrow terms. In the workplace, key performance indicators (KPIs) reduce creativity and innovation to quantifiable outputs. And in healthcare, patients are often defined by their lab results rather than their lived experiences.

Jerry Muller, in his book *The Tyranny of Metrics*, critiques this obsession with measurement. He argues that while metrics can provide valuable insights, they often distort the very systems they're meant to improve. By prioritizing what is easy to measure over what is meaningful, we create environments that reward gaming the system rather than genuine growth or progress.

I've felt the weight of metrics in almost every aspect of my life. In school, my grades often felt like a judgment of my worth rather than a reflection of my abilities. At work, performance reviews seemed to prioritize appearances over actual impact. And in healthcare, the constant focus on test results left me feeling unseen and unheard. The metrics didn't capture my creativity, my resilience, or my humanity—they only measured how well I fit the system's predefined standards.

Albert Einstein once said, "Not everything that can be counted counts, and not everything that counts can be counted." This truth lies at the heart of the problem with Strive metrics. They quantify the quantifiable but overlook the immeasurable qualities that make us human.

The Cost of Over-Measurement

The cost of over-measurement is more than personal—it's systemic. By prioritizing metrics over meaning, we create systems that reward compliance and discourage innovation. In education, this means students who focus on passing tests rather than pursuing their passions. In the workplace, it means employees who prioritize short-term goals over long-term impact. And in healthcare, it means doctors who treat lab results rather than patients.

Viktor Frankl, in *Man's Search for Meaning*, reminds us that "success cannot be pursued; it must ensue." This insight challenges the core logic of Strive metrics. Success isn't something we achieve by meeting benchmarks—it's something we experience when we align our actions with our values and purpose.

One of the most profound lessons I've learned through my journey with chronic illness and neurodivergence is that true success often lies outside the bounds of measurable outcomes. When I was at my lowest—struggling with symptoms of EDS and POTS, navigating a system that refused to see me—I realized that my worth wasn't defined by my ability to meet the metrics. It was defined by my resilience, my creativity, and my connection to others.

The Growth Mindset

Carol Dweck's work on the growth mindset offers a powerful alternative to the rigidity of Strive metrics. Dweck distinguishes between a fixed mindset, which sees abilities as static and unchangeable, and a growth mindset, which sees challenges as opportunities for learning and development. Thrive systems embrace the growth mindset, valuing progress over perfection and effort over outcomes.

In education, this means creating environments where students are encouraged to take risks, make mistakes, and learn from failure. In the workplace, it means valuing innovation and experimentation over adherence to rigid processes. And in healthcare, it means treating patients as partners in their care, valuing their experiences and insights alongside clinical data.

I've seen the power of the growth mindset in my own life. When I shifted my focus from meeting external metrics to pursuing my own goals and values, I began to thrive in ways I never thought possible. This didn't mean ignoring the challenges I faced—it meant approaching them with curiosity and creativity rather than fear and frustration.

Redefining Success

Breaking free of Strive metrics requires us to redefine success in ways that align with the principles of Thrive. Success isn't about meeting arbitrary benchmarks—it's about creating environments where individuals and communities can flourish.

Kate Raworth's *Doughnut Economics* offers a compelling framework for this redefinition. Raworth argues that success should be measured not by GDP or other narrow metrics, but by whether we're meeting the social needs of all people while staying within the ecological limits of the planet. This shift from growth to balance reflects the core values of Thrive: abundance, interdependence, and resilience.

Brené Brown echoes this sentiment in her work on vulnerability and connection. She writes, "Daring leaders work to make sure people can show up, be seen, and be heard without fear of judgment." This is the essence of Thrive systems: creating spaces where people can bring their whole selves, free from the constraints of Strive metrics.

A Personal Reflection

As I reflect on my own journey, I think about how much of my life has been shaped by metrics—grades, performance reviews, lab results. For years, I let these numbers define me, believing that my worth was tied to how well I met the system's standards. But over time, I've come to see that these metrics are just one piece of a much larger puzzle.

True success, for me, has been about finding meaning in the midst of uncertainty. It's been about connecting with others, embracing my creativity, and learning to see my challenges as opportunities for growth. These are the things that can't be measured by tests or scores, but they are the things that matter most.

The Promise of Breaking Free

Breaking free of Strive metrics is not just about rejecting old standards—it's about creating new ones that reflect the values of Thrive. It's about measuring what matters: connection, creativity, and community. And it's about recognizing that success isn't something we achieve alone—it's something we build together.

As we continue this journey, I invite you to reflect on your own relationship with metrics. Where have they constrained you? And what would it look like to define success on your own terms?

Chapter 12: The Role of AI in Thrive

Artificial intelligence is transforming our world at an unprecedented pace. From automating mundane tasks to revolutionizing entire industries, AI has the potential to free us from repetitive labor and create new opportunities for creativity and connection. But like any powerful tool, AI's impact depends on how we use it. Will it reinforce the scarcity-driven, fear-based systems of Strive, or will it help us build the abundance-focused, interdependent systems of Thrive?

The rise of AI offers a unique moment to rethink our systems and design a future that prioritizes well-being over efficiency, collaboration over competition, and creativity over compliance.

AI in Strive Systems

In Strive systems, AI is often deployed to maximize productivity, enforce control, and reduce costs. Algorithms are used to monitor employees, predict consumer behavior, and optimize supply chains—all with the goal of increasing efficiency. While these applications can deliver short-term benefits, they often come at the expense of human dignity and connection.

Michel Foucault's concept of the *panopticon* is particularly relevant here. Foucault described the panopticon as a structure of surveillance that enforces compliance through the fear of being watched. AI, when used in Strive systems, becomes a digital panopticon, monitoring every action and decision to ensure conformity. In workplaces, this can look like constant tracking of performance metrics. In education, it can mean the rise of AI-driven testing systems that reduce students to data points. And in healthcare, it can mean prioritizing algorithms over empathy.

I've felt the weight of these systems in my own life. When I worked in environments that relied heavily on metrics and surveillance, I often felt like a cog in a machine rather than a person. The pressure to meet targets and conform to rigid expectations left little room for creativity or autonomy. AI, in these contexts, didn't feel like a tool for empowerment—it felt like a tool for control.

AI in Thrive Systems

But AI doesn't have to reinforce Strive systems. It can also be a powerful enabler of Thrive systems, creating environments where people have the freedom to explore, connect, and grow. The key lies in how we design and deploy these technologies.

Daniel Pink's framework of autonomy, mastery, and purpose provides a useful lens for thinking about AI in Thrive systems. Imagine an AI-driven workplace that uses technology to enhance autonomy by automating repetitive tasks, giving employees more time to focus on creative and meaningful work. Or consider an educational system where AI personalizes learning experiences, helping students explore their unique interests and strengths. In healthcare, AI could be used to analyze complex data, freeing up doctors to spend more time listening to their patients.

Kate Raworth's *Doughnut Economics* also offers insights into how AI can align with the principles of Thrive. Raworth emphasizes the importance of designing systems that operate within ecological and social boundaries. AI, when used responsibly, can help us achieve this balance by optimizing resource use, reducing waste, and supporting sustainable practices.

The Risks of AI in Thrive

Despite its potential, AI also poses significant risks. If not carefully managed, it could exacerbate inequality, reinforce biases, and entrench the power of Strive systems. Algorithms, after all, are only as good as the data they're trained on—and when that data reflects existing inequalities, the outcomes often do, too.

Brené Brown's work on vulnerability and trust reminds us that technology is only as ethical as the people who design and use it. "Trust is built in small moments," she writes, emphasizing the importance of human connection in a world increasingly shaped by technology. To ensure AI supports Thrive systems, we must prioritize transparency, accountability, and inclusion in its development and deployment.

Personal Reflections on AI

For me, the rise of AI has been both exciting and unsettling. As someone who values creativity and autonomy, I see the potential for AI to free us from mundane tasks and open up new possibilities for exploration and growth. But I've also experienced the ways technology can feel dehumanizing, particularly in systems that prioritize efficiency over empathy.

I remember one experience with an AI-driven healthcare platform that promised to streamline the diagnostic process. While the platform was efficient, it left me feeling more like a data point than a person. My symptoms, which didn't fit neatly into predefined categories, were flagged as "inconclusive," and the system offered no space for nuance or context. It was a stark reminder that technology, while powerful, cannot replace the human connection that lies at the heart of care.

But I've also seen glimpses of what AI can do when used thoughtfully. I've connected with online communities where AI tools help people with chronic illnesses track their symptoms, identify patterns, and advocate for themselves more effectively. These tools don't replace human connection—they enhance it, creating new opportunities for collaboration and support.

The Wild Potential of AI

The Wild offers a compelling metaphor for what AI could be in Thrive systems. In the Wild, every organism has a role to play, and the system thrives on diversity and balance. AI, when used to support abundance, interdependence, and resilience, can help us create human systems that mirror these qualities.

For example, AI could be used to model sustainable practices, helping communities manage shared resources in ways that benefit everyone. It could facilitate global collaboration, connecting people across cultures and disciplines to solve complex challenges. And it could enhance our understanding of ourselves and our world, providing new tools for learning, creativity, and connection.

Viktor Frankl's insight that "when we are no longer able to change a situation, we are challenged to change ourselves" feels especially relevant here. AI is not a solution in itself—it's a tool that reflects our values and choices. To create a future where AI supports Thrive, we must challenge ourselves to think differently about technology and its role in our lives.

A Call to Action

The role of AI in Thrive is not predetermined—it's a choice. It's a choice about how we design, deploy, and use technology to shape our systems and our futures. As we continue this journey, I invite you to reflect on your own relationship with AI. Where has it constrained you? Where has it empowered you? And what role will you play in ensuring that AI supports a world where everyone has the freedom to thrive?

Chapter 13: Emotional Resilience and Collective Striving

Resilience is often viewed as an individual trait—the ability to bounce back from adversity, to endure hardships, to find strength in the face of uncertainty. But true resilience is not something we develop alone. It's a collective practice, deeply rooted in the connections we build and the support systems we create. In a Thrive system, resilience is not about survival—it's about thriving together.

The Role of Emotional Resilience

Emotional resilience is the foundation of collective striving. Brené Brown defines resilience as "the ability to move through discomfort and vulnerability with courage." This courage doesn't come from isolation—it comes from connection. It's in our shared experiences, our mutual support, and our willingness to show up for one another that we find the strength to endure and grow.

In Strive systems, resilience is often framed as a personal responsibility. We're told to work harder, to push through, to "grit" our way to success. But this narrative ignores the systemic barriers that make resilience necessary in the first place. It places the burden of survival on individuals while leaving the structures of oppression and scarcity intact.

For me, this framing has often felt like a double-edged sword. As someone navigating chronic illness and neurodivergence, I've had to develop resilience to survive in systems that weren't designed for me. But I've also felt the weight of the expectation to endure without support. It wasn't until I found communities that valued connection over competition that I began to experience resilience as a shared practice rather than an individual burden.

The Cost of Isolation

The isolation fostered by Strive systems comes at a profound cost. Viktor Frankl, in *Man's Search for Meaning*, wrote, "When we are no longer able to change a situation, we are challenged to change ourselves." While this insight speaks to the power of individual resilience, it also highlights the need for connection. Without support, the burden of change can become overwhelming.

In education, isolation manifests as students who feel unseen and unsupported. In the workplace, it's employees who are left to navigate burnout alone. And in healthcare, it's patients who are dismissed or ignored when they don't fit into the system's predefined categories. This isolation is not a failure of individuals—it's a failure of the systems that surround them.

I've felt this isolation acutely in the healthcare system. When my symptoms of EDS and POTS didn't align with standard diagnostic frameworks, I was left to advocate for myself in an environment that often felt hostile. The lack of understanding and support was exhausting, but it also reinforced the importance of connection. It was the communities of others facing similar challenges that gave me the strength to keep going.

The Power of Collective Striving

Collective striving is the antidote to isolation. It's the practice of working together to overcome challenges, to support one another, and to build systems that prioritize connection and care. This collective approach is rooted in the principles of Thrive: abundance, interdependence, and resilience.

Elinor Ostrom's research on the commons offers a powerful model for collective striving. Ostrom demonstrated that communities can sustainably manage shared resources when they prioritize collaboration, trust, and shared responsibility. This same principle applies to resilience. When we work together, we create networks of support that allow everyone to thrive.

Brené Brown's work on vulnerability also underscores the importance of connection in resilience. She writes, "Vulnerability is not winning or losing; it's having the courage to show up when you can't control the outcome." In collective striving, this vulnerability becomes a source of strength. It allows us to build relationships based on trust, empathy, and mutual support.

Resilience in the Wild

The Wild offers a powerful metaphor for resilience. In natural ecosystems, resilience is not an individual trait—it's a property of the system as a whole. Forests recover from fires, rivers adapt to changing flows, and species evolve to meet new challenges. This resilience is not about perfection or invulnerability—it's about balance, diversity, and interconnection.

In human systems, resilience in the Wild means creating environments where people can lean on one another, where failure is seen as a stepping stone to growth, and where diversity is celebrated as a source of strength. It's about designing systems that adapt and evolve in response to change, rather than breaking under pressure.

For me, the Wild represents the kind of resilience I've found in the communities that have supported me through my health challenges. These communities didn't ask me to "grit" my way through adversity—they offered me resources, understanding, and care. They reminded me that resilience isn't about going it alone—it's about thriving together.

A Personal Reflection

As I reflect on my own journey, I think about the moments when resilience felt like an impossible burden. I think about the doctors who dismissed my symptoms, the workplaces that valued metrics over well-being, and the systems that left me to navigate challenges alone. But I also think about the moments when resilience became a shared practice. I think about the friends who supported me, the communities that embraced me, and the connections that gave me strength.

These experiences have taught me that resilience is not just an individual trait—it's a collective one. It's something we build together, through trust, empathy, and mutual support. And it's something we can design into our systems, creating environments where everyone has the opportunity to thrive.

The Promise of Collective Resilience

Collective resilience is the foundation of Thrive. It challenges the isolation of Strive systems and offers a vision of connection, collaboration, and care. It asks us to move beyond individual success to create environments where everyone can flourish.

As we continue this journey, I invite you to reflect on your own experiences with resilience. Where have you felt the weight of isolation? And what would it look like to create a world where resilience is a shared practice, rooted in connection and care?

Chapter 14: Returning to the Commons

Throughout history, the commons have been a vital source of abundance, connection, and resilience. These shared resources—whether forests, fisheries, or cultural knowledge—are the foundation of thriving communities. But Strive systems, with their emphasis on privatization and competition, have eroded the commons, replacing collective stewardship with individual ownership and scarcity. To transition from Strive to Thrive, we must reclaim the commons, rediscovering the power of shared resources and collective care.

The Erosion of the Commons

The erosion of the commons is one of the defining features of Strive systems. Elinor Ostrom's groundbreaking research challenged the assumption that shared resources are doomed to overuse and destruction, a concept famously known as the "tragedy of the commons." Ostrom demonstrated that communities can sustainably manage shared resources through cooperation, trust, and locally adapted rules. Her work stands as a powerful counterpoint to the narrative that privatization is the only way to prevent scarcity.

Yet, despite Ostrom's insights, Strive systems have continued to dismantle the commons. Public spaces are sold to private developers. Knowledge is locked behind paywalls. Natural resources are exploited for profit rather than preserved for future generations. This erosion of the commons doesn't just harm the environment—it undermines our ability to connect, collaborate, and thrive as a society.

I've felt the impact of this erosion in my own life. When I was struggling with my health, I often turned to online communities for support and information. These spaces, built on the principles of the commons, were a lifeline for me. But I also saw how the privatization of knowledge—through medical gatekeeping, expensive treatments, and inaccessible research—created barriers that made it harder for people like me to find the care and support we needed.

The Power of the Commons

Reclaiming the commons is not just about restoring resources—it's about rebuilding relationships. As Ostrom's work shows, the strength of the commons lies in the trust, cooperation, and shared responsibility of the communities that steward them. These principles align perfectly with the core values of Thrive: abundance, interdependence, and resilience.

In the natural world, the commons are everywhere. Forests, rivers, and oceans function as shared resources, sustaining countless species and ecosystems. In human systems, the commons take many forms: public libraries, open-source software, community gardens, and even the Internet. These shared spaces and resources create opportunities for connection, collaboration, and creativity.

Howard Gardner's theory of multiple intelligences reminds us that the commons are not just physical—they are also intellectual and cultural. Knowledge, art, and traditions are forms of the commons that enrich our lives and expand our understanding of the world. When we share these resources freely, we create a culture of abundance that benefits everyone.

Reclaiming the Commons

Reclaiming the commons requires us to challenge the scarcity mindset that underpins Strive systems. It means resisting the privatization of resources and advocating for policies that prioritize collective well-being over individual profit. It also means reimagining how we design and steward shared spaces, ensuring they are accessible, inclusive, and sustainable.

Kate Raworth's *Doughnut Economics* offers a powerful framework for this reimagining. Raworth argues that the goal of economic systems should be to meet the needs of all people while staying within the ecological limits of the planet. This balance requires a strong commitment to the commons, from protecting public lands to investing in renewable energy and open-source technology.

One of the most inspiring examples of reclaiming the commons comes from the global movement for open access to scientific research. Organizations like Creative Commons have made it possible for knowledge to be shared freely, breaking down barriers and democratizing access to information. This movement embodies the principles of abundance, interdependence, and resilience, showing us what's possible when we prioritize the collective good.

A Personal Reflection

The commons have played a significant role in my own journey. When I was navigating the challenges of EDS and POTS, it was the commons—online communities, shared knowledge, and collective support—that gave me hope and direction. These spaces reminded me that I wasn't alone, that my experiences mattered, and that there were people who cared about helping one another thrive.

But I've also seen the fragility of the commons. I've seen how easily they can be eroded by privatization, exclusion, and neglect. And I've felt the frustration of navigating systems that prioritize profit over people, making it harder for individuals and communities to access the resources they need to flourish.

Brené Brown writes, "We don't have to do it alone. We were never meant to." This truth lies at the heart of the commons. They are not just resources—they are relationships, built on trust, empathy, and mutual care. Reclaiming the commons means reclaiming our connection to one another and to the world around us.

The Wild as a Commons

The Wild offers a powerful metaphor for the commons. In the Wild, resources are not owned—they are shared. Forests provide shelter, rivers sustain life, and ecosystems thrive on the balance and interdependence of their members. This model of abundance and connection is the foundation of Thrive systems.

In human terms, the Wild as a commons means creating systems that prioritize collaboration over competition, sustainability over extraction, and connection over isolation. It means designing cities that balance urban development with green spaces, creating workplaces that prioritize well-being over profit, and building communities that celebrate diversity and inclusion.

A Call to Reclaim

Reclaiming the commons is not just a political or economic challenge—it's a cultural one. It asks us to move beyond the individualism of Strive systems and embrace the collective spirit of Thrive. It asks us to see ourselves not as isolated individuals, but as members of a shared ecosystem, deeply connected to one another and to the world.

As we continue this journey, I invite you to reflect on your own relationship with the commons. Where have you experienced their power? Where have you seen their erosion? And what role will you play in reclaiming and stewarding the commons for future generations?

Chapter 15: The Lion's Roar

In the wilderness, the lion's roar is a symbol of strength, confidence, and connection. It's not just a declaration of presence—it's a call to the community, a reminder that the lion belongs to something larger than itself. As we conclude this journey through Thrive, the lion's roar serves as a metaphor for the courage it takes to embrace abundance, interdependence, and resilience in a world still dominated by Strive systems. It's a reminder that thriving is not a solitary act—it's a collective one.

Balancing Autonomy, Mastery, and Belonging

Daniel Pink's *Drive* introduced us to the pillars of autonomy, mastery, and purpose as the foundation of motivation. Thrive builds on this framework, emphasizing that these pillars cannot exist in isolation—they must be balanced within systems that support connection and community.

Autonomy is essential for creativity and self-expression, but without connection, it can become isolation. Mastery drives innovation and growth, but without collaboration, it can lead to competition and burnout. Belonging fosters trust and resilience, but without autonomy, it can feel like conformity. Thrive systems recognize this balance, creating environments where individuals and communities can flourish together.

For me, this balance has been a lifelong struggle. As someone who values autonomy deeply, I've often resisted the structures of belonging that felt confining or conditional. But I've also experienced the profound joy of connection—of being part of a community that values my unique contributions while supporting my growth. It's this balance, between individuality and interdependence, that lies at the heart of Thrive.

The Courage to Roar

The lion's roar is not just a metaphor for thriving—it's a call to action. It takes courage to embrace Thrive principles in a world that rewards scarcity, control, and competition. It takes courage to challenge the systems that stifle creativity, marginalize difference, and prioritize profit over people. And it takes courage to believe in abundance, to trust in connection, and to commit to resilience.

Brené Brown reminds us that "courage starts with showing up and letting ourselves be seen." This vulnerability is the foundation of the lion's roar. It's the willingness to stand up for what we believe in, to take risks, and to create spaces where others can do the same.

I think about the moments in my own life when I've had to find the courage to roar. Whether it was advocating for myself in the healthcare system, challenging outdated norms in the workplace, or building connections in online communities, these moments required me to step outside my comfort zone and trust in the power of my voice.

But I also think about the people who have roared for me—who have believed in me when I couldn't believe in myself. Brian Stearns, with his unwavering support, reminded me of my own strength and potential. His belief in me echoes the story of Mike Williams and Les Brown, a reminder that sometimes the greatest gift we can give one another is the courage to roar.

The Collective Roar

In Thrive systems, the lion's roar is not a solitary act—it's a collective one. It's the sound of communities coming together to challenge Strive systems and create environments where everyone can flourish. It's the courage of students demanding better education, of workers advocating for fair treatment, and of communities reclaiming the commons.

Elinor Ostrom's work on the commons provides a powerful model for this collective roar. Ostrom demonstrated that communities thrive when they prioritize trust, cooperation, and shared responsibility. This same principle applies to the systems we build. When we come together to create, innovate, and connect, we amplify one another's voices and create a roar that cannot be ignored.

This collective roar is what I've witnessed in online communities of individuals with chronic illnesses, neurodivergence, and other marginalized identities. These communities have shown me what's possible when we move beyond competition and isolation to embrace connection and collaboration. They are a testament to the power of the lion's roar—not as a declaration of dominance, but as a call to thrive together.

A Reflection on Belief

As I reflect on this journey, I am struck by the profound importance of belief—not just belief in ourselves, but belief in one another. Brian's belief in me gave me the courage to keep going when everything felt impossible. And Mike Williams's belief in Les Brown reminds us that sometimes we need someone else's faith in us to ignite our own.

In the spirit of the lion's roar, I want to share this belief with you. I believe in your potential to thrive, to create, and to connect. I believe in your ability to challenge the systems that hold us back and to build a future rooted in abundance, interdependence, and resilience. And I believe in our collective power to create a world where everyone has the freedom to flourish.

The Call to Thrive

The lion's roar is not the end of the journey—it's the beginning. It's a call to reimagine our systems, to reconnect with one another, and to reclaim the Wild as a space of creativity, connection, and growth. It's a reminder that thriving is not just a possibility—it's a choice.

As we conclude this journey, I leave you with one final question: What will you do to answer the call? How will you roar?

Epilogue: The Thrive Collective

As we stand on the threshold of change, it's clear that Thrive is not just a theory—it's a choice. A choice to move beyond the limitations of Strive systems, to embrace abundance, interdependence, and resilience, and to build a future where everyone has the freedom to flourish. But this choice is not one we can make alone. It requires collective action, shared vision, and a commitment to creating systems that reflect our deepest values.

The Power of Community and Belief

Throughout this journey, we've explored the principles of Thrive and the systems that support it. But none of these principles—abundance, interdependence, resilience—can exist without community. As Brené Brown reminds us, "Connection is why we're here; it is what gives purpose and meaning to our lives." The Thrive Collective is an invitation to build that connection—to come together as individuals, communities, and systems to create a world where everyone can thrive.

For me, the power of community has been a constant source of strength. When I faced the challenges of chronic illness, neurodivergence, and systemic barriers, it was the support of others that helped me keep going. Friends like Brian Stearns reminded me of my own strength and potential when I couldn't see it myself. His belief in me was a turning point, much like the story of Les Brown and Mike Williams.

If you're unfamiliar with Les Brown, let me take a moment to introduce him. Les Brown is one of the most celebrated motivational speakers in the world, renowned for his ability to inspire audiences with his story of resilience and triumph. Born in Liberty City, Miami, Les was labeled "educably mentally retarded" as a child and placed in special education classes. Yet, with the encouragement of mentors and his unrelenting belief in himself, he rose above those early limitations to become a prominent voice in personal development and success.

Les often tells the story of his early struggles and how his mentor, Mike Williams, played a pivotal role in his journey. Mike saw something in Les that he couldn't yet see in himself, pushing him to take risks, embrace his potential, and believe in his ability to inspire others. "You've got greatness within you," Mike would tell him—a phrase that became a mantra for Les and millions of people worldwide who've been touched by his work.

The Parallels to My Story

Brian's role in my life echoes Mike's role in Les's. When I was at my lowest, feeling defeated by systems that seemed designed to hold me back, Brian's belief in me gave me the courage to keep going. He reminded me that I had value, that my voice mattered, and that I could not only survive but thrive—and that I could help others do the same.

This connection between Les's story and my own highlights a profound truth: belief is transformative. It's not just a gift we give to ourselves—it's a gift we give to one another. Just as Mike's belief sparked Les's journey, and Brian's belief reignited mine, I hope this book serves as a spark for you—a reminder that you, too, have greatness within you.

The Thrive Collective: A Vision for the Future

The Thrive Collective is more than an idea—it's a call to action. It's a global community dedicated to reimagining systems and creating environments where everyone has the opportunity to flourish. The Collective is grounded in three core principles:

1. **Abundance**: Sharing resources, ideas, and opportunities to create a culture of collaboration and creativity.
2. **Interdependence**: Building trust, empathy, and connection to foster resilience and mutual support.
3. **Resilience**: Embracing change, learning from failure, and growing stronger together.

Through the Thrive Collective, we can create spaces where people from all walks of life can come together to share their experiences, collaborate on solutions, and support one another in the journey to thrive. Whether it's through local initiatives, online communities, or global movements, the Collective is a space where connection and creativity are celebrated.

An Invitation to Join

You don't have to be an expert or a leader to be part of the Thrive Collective. All you need is the willingness to show up, to listen, and to contribute in whatever way feels meaningful to you. Whether it's sharing your story, supporting others, or taking action in your community, your voice matters.

To join the Thrive Collective, email me at michaelrhettmccarthy@gmail.com. Together, we can build a network of support and inspiration that spans borders, disciplines, and perspectives.

A Personal Reflection

The parallels between Les Brown's story and my own remind me of the profound importance of belief—not just belief in ourselves, but belief in one another. When Mike Williams told Les he had greatness within him, it wasn't just encouragement—it was a catalyst that transformed Les's self-perception and set him on a path to greatness. In the same way, Brian's belief in me wasn't just support—it was a lifeline that reminded me of my own potential at a time when I felt lost.

This book has been an effort to pay that belief forward. It's a reflection of my own journey, but it's also an invitation for you to embark on yours. Just as Mike believed in Les, and Brian believed in me, I believe in you. I believe in your potential to create, to connect, and to thrive. And I believe in our collective power to transform systems that stifle us into systems that set us free.

The Final Call to Thrive

Thrive is not just a destination—it's a journey. It's a choice we make every day to build systems that honor our humanity, our creativity, and our connection to one another. It's a commitment to move beyond survival and scarcity, to embrace the Wild as a space of possibility and growth.

As Aldo Leopold once said, "Harmony with land is like harmony with a friend; you cannot cherish his right hand and chop off his left." The same is true of our systems. We cannot thrive in systems that ask us to merely survive. We must build systems that honor the whole—our communities, our planet, and ourselves.

So I leave you with this question: What will you do to help us move from the farm, escape the zoo, and embrace the wild? What role will you play in building the Thrive Collective?

The journey begins here, and it begins with us. Let's thrive—together.

References

Brown, Brené. *Daring Greatly: How the Courage to Be Vulnerable Transforms the Way We Live, Love, Parent, and Lead.* Gotham Books, 2012.

Butler, Judith. *Gender Trouble: Feminism and the Subversion of Identity.* Routledge, 1990.

Einstein, Albert. Quoted in "Education is What Remains…" Multiple Sources.

Frankl, Viktor E. *Man's Search for Meaning.* Beacon Press, 2006.

Foucault, Michel. *Discipline and Punish: The Birth of the Prison.* Translated by Alan Sheridan, Vintage Books, 1995.

Gardner, Howard. *Frames of Mind: The Theory of Multiple Intelligences.* Basic Books, 1983.

Leopold, Aldo. *A Sand County Almanac: And Sketches Here and There.* Oxford University Press, 1949.

Les Brown. *Live Your Dreams: Say "Yes" to Life.* Morrow, 1992.

Muller, Jerry Z. *The Tyranny of Metrics.* Princeton University Press, 2018.

Ostrom, Elinor. *Governing the Commons: The Evolution of Institutions for Collective Action.* Cambridge University Press, 1990.

Pink, Daniel H. *Drive: The Surprising Truth About What Motivates Us.* Riverhead Books, 2009.

Raworth, Kate. *Doughnut Economics: Seven Ways to Think Like a 21st-Century Economist.* Chelsea Green Publishing, 2017.

Scott, James C. *Seeing Like a State: How Certain Schemes to Improve the Human Condition Have Failed.* Yale University Press, 1998.

www.ingramcontent.com/pod-product-compliance
Lightning Source LLC
Chambersburg PA
CBHW071056240526
45469CB00006BD/2320